WAITING FOR SINTERKLAAS

A FAMILY IN THE NETHERLANDS

Hélène Tremblay

Peguis Publishers   Winnipeg, Canada

97 98 99 00 01 5 4 3 2 1

Canadian Cataloguing in Publication Data
Tremblay, Hélène

　　　Waiting for Sinterklaas
　　　(Families of the world)

ISBN 1-894110-05-6

1. Family - Netherlands - Juvenile literature.
2. Netherlands - Social life and customs - Juvenile
literature. I. Title. II. Series: Tremblay, Hélène.
Families of the world

HQ636.T745 1997　　306.85'09492　　C97-920141-1

Adapted for young readers by Peguis Publishers
Book design by Bill Stewart
Printed and bound in Canada by Friesens
Drawings by Pamela Dixon
Photographs by Hélène Tremblay except:
　　　Windmill, p.13, by H. Kurihara/Tony Stone Images.
　　　Canal, p.31, by J. Lawrence/Tony Stone Images.
　　　Bikes, p.17, and tulips, p.30, courtesy of the
　　　Netherlands Board of Tourism.

Story on pp. 24–25 adapted from "The Hero of Haarlem"
in *Hans Brinker, or The Silver Skates* by Mary Mapes Dodge.

Maps by Magellan Geographix[SM] Santa Barbara, CA
World Map©1994, Netherlands Map©1992

PEGUIS PUBLISHERS
100-318 McDermot Avenue
Winnipeg, Manitoba
Canada R3A 0A2
1-800-667-9673

CONTENTS

The Oltheten-Pelder Family:
1 - Marthe (11 months), **2** - Helen (Mother, 34),
3 - Douwe (3), **4** - Michel (Father, 37),
5 - Dennis (5)

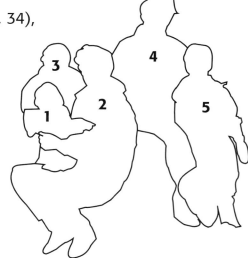

INTRODUCTION

Families around the world have special times together. In the Netherlands, the Christmas season is a special time of the year. Excitement for children begins in late November when Sinterklaas [SIN-ter-klahs] and Zwarte Piet [ZWAR-teh peet] come to town. In this story, you will meet the Oltheten-Pelder family. They are getting ready for St. Nicholas Eve on December 5.

Sinterklaas and Zwarte Piet wait to greet the children.

WAITING FOR SINTERKLAAS

Saturday, December 3

Douwe [DOE-ee] and Dennis cannot sit still. It will soon be St. Nicholas Eve. That's the night Sinterklaas brings presents to all good boys and girls. "Just two more days," their mother tells them. To the boys, however, even one more day seems like forever.

Sinterklaas, Zwarte Piet, and their helpers arrive in the Netherlands about 3 weeks before St. Nicholas Day. They travel to all the towns and cities visiting the children.

At this time of year, Douwe and Dennis are on their best behavior. They know Sinterklaas only gives presents to children who have been good. He gives chunks of coal to children who have been bad. And they've even heard stories of how Zwarte Piet's helpers stuff bad children into big bags and take them away from their families. So, Douwe and Dennis try to be extra good. They go to bed when they are told. They share their toys with each other. Dennis even helps Helen wash the dishes.

Sinterklaas

Sinterklaas to Dutch children is like Santa Claus to North American children. But there are some differences. Sinterklaas comes from Spain, not the North Pole. He travels by steamboat, not by sleigh and reindeer. He arrives in the middle of November, not in December and stays for about 3 weeks. He has a <u>traveling companion</u> named Zwarte Piet who is a <u>Moor</u>. Zwarte Piet always brings lots of helpers with him.

When Sinterklaas and Zwarte Piet arrive in Amsterdam on the steamboat, they are greeted by the mayor and hundreds of children. Then Sinterklaas rides on a white horse through streets lined with even more children. Zwarte Piet and his helpers walk beside Sinterklaas and throw candies to the crowds of children. From the time of their arrival until St. Nicholas Eve, Sinterklaas and Zwarte Piet travel from town to town. They visit children throughout the Netherlands.

Today, to help pass the time, Michel suggests they all go for a walk. Michel, Helen, and the children like the outdoors at any time of the year. The nearby forest is one of their favorite places to spend an afternoon together. The sky is gray, and the air is cool. But it is not too cold for a walk in the woods. Everyone dresses warmly in sweaters and jackets. Helen bundles Marthe in her snowsuit.

Michel and Helen spend as much time as they can with their children. They talk to them about many things. On their walk through the woods,

Michel, Helen, and the children like being outdoors at any time of the year. One of their favorite places for a walk is in the forest near their home.

Michel tells his sons how birds and small animals need the forest for their homes and food. He explains how important it is for people to protect and respect the <u>environment</u>. That way, birds and animals and people can enjoy <u>nature</u> for many, many years.

Dennis and Douwe climb over a tree that has been cut down.

When they reach the stream, Dennis lets go of his father's hand and shuffles through the leaves. Douwe runs after him. Baby Marthe loves the crunchy sound the leaves make as her brothers run around. She laughs and claps her hands. Next, the boys find a pile of logs to climb over. Michel shows them how to count the rings in the <u>stumps</u> to find out how old the tree is.

Michel cares about the environment. He tells his children how important it is to protect the forest for the birds and animals that live there.

It is late afternoon by the time the family arrives back home. They live on a busy street in a tall, narrow house. Helen and Michel have a bedroom on the third floor of their house. Marthe sleeps in a crib in the corner of their room. Douwe and Dennis each have a bedroom on the second floor. The kitchen, living room, and dining room are on the main floor. Their home is small and they have many stairs to climb. They don't have a garage or a basement. They have to store their bicycles, tricycles, and Marthe's stroller in the hallway on the main floor.

Michel, Helen, and their children live on this street in a big city called The Hague. Their house is tall, narrow, and deep, like many houses in the Netherlands.

Michel and Helen sometimes think about moving to a bigger house. If they lived in a newer house in the suburbs, they would have a lot more space. Helen would also have a big yard where she could grow fruits and vegetables in the summer. But, they always decide to stay where they are. They live close to downtown, Michel's workplace, and the children's school.

Helen and Michel also like their neighborhood because it is home to people from many countries around the world. A family from Romania lives on one side of them. A family from Vietnam lives on the other side. A Turkish family lives behind them. Helen and Michel think it is important for their children to learn about people from different places.

The hallway on the main floor of the house is very narrow. It is often cluttered with bicycles.

In the Netherlands, most older houses are tall and narrow. When these city houses were built hundreds of years ago, they could only be three windows wide. There was a shortage of land everywhere, especially by the canals, so most homes were built side by side to save space.

Sunday, December 4

Today, the family is going to the seashore. Although they live near the center of the city, the North Sea is only a fifteen-minute drive away.

Helen sets Marthe in her highchair. By the time the coffee is ready, the boys are bounding down the stairs. Helen serves a hearty breakfast, called *ontbijt* [ont-BAYD], of bread, cheese, peanut butter, and honey. Today, the boys are even more excited. Only one more day until St. Nicholas Eve!

Michel packs the stroller, two fishing rods, and a fishing net in the trunk of the car. Everyone piles into the car and they drive to the seashore.

Helen makes sure everyone eats a hearty breakfast before they go to the seashore.

Land Reclamation

In the Netherlands, there are <u>sea walls</u> and <u>dikes</u> almost everywhere along the coast. These help keep the North Sea from flooding the land. That is because at least a third of the country is below sea level.

Hundreds of years ago, much of the western part of present-day Netherlands was under water. When the people decided to <u>reclaim</u> the land from the sea, they did it in several steps. First, they built dikes around the water-covered land they were reclaiming. Next, they set up pumps and built windmills to power the pumps. They needed to pump the water out of the diked area until dry land, called a polder, appeared. Then, they built canals to drain the water into the sea. Because of rain and <u>seepage</u>, polders have to be pumped continuously. Today, modern machines, not windmills, do the pumping.

Many cities, including Amsterdam and The Hague, are built on polders.

As soon as they arrive at the sea, the boys run down to the sandy beach. They <u>wade</u> into the cold, shallow water. Thick woolen socks keep their feet warm in their rubber boots. They spend the morning walking along the shoreline, looking for small sea creatures and interesting shells.

Early in the afternoon, Helen calls Douwe and Dennis to her and gives them the snacks she has packed. Everyone bites into big red apples. Then Helen carefully unwraps a special treat, a Dutch

Dennis and Douwe walk along the seashore looking for sea creatures.

chocolate bar filled with raisins and nuts. Later, they all climb up on the sea wall. Michel shows Dennis how to throw his fishing line into the water. They wait patiently, but fishing is too slow for Dennis. He would rather play along the sea wall and chase the gulls that fly overhead. Helen helps Douwe hold his fishing rod over the rail. He is tired and is happy to stay still for a while.

Helen makes sure baby Marthe is warmly snuggled in her snowsuit.

While Michel and Dennis walk farther along the sea wall to watch gulls, Helen helps Douwe try to catch some fish.

In the evening the family sits down to a light dinner. The boys are already in their pyjamas, ready for bed. They have to be up early for school tomorrow.

Michel reads the boys a bedtime story and tucks them into bed. Then he goes back downstairs and sits at the table with his desktop computer. He is designing invitations for a Christmas play. He and Helen and some other parents are putting on a play. They will perform it at the boys' school in a couple of weeks.

Michel uses his computer for many things. On this evening, he is designing invitations for a Christmas play.

The family sits down to a light supper. Marthe and the boys are already in their pyjamas, ready for bed.

Monday, December 5

Michel eats his breakfast before the rest of the family is up. Then he hops on his bicycle. He rides to work on the bike path that runs alongside the heavy traffic. Even though almost everyone has a bicycle, there are six million cars in this small country. The Netherlands is the most crowded country in Europe. And, like all <u>industrial</u> countries, there is a lot of pollution. Michel and Helen worry about the kind of world their children are growing up in.

Michel works for a big company. His job is to help businesses and the government find ways to clean up air and water pollution. For example, the government has built bicycle paths throughout the country. Many people, like Michel, now leave their cars at home and ride their bicycles to work. The country also has a well-organized public transportation system that a lot of people use.

Douwe and Dennis are already awake when Helen opens their bedroom doors. They are excited. Today is St. Nicholas Eve!

Most Dutch children don't start school until they are five years old. But Dennis and Douwe attend an alternative school. They have classes from 8:00 a.m. until noon. Helen and Michel, along with some other parents, started their own school. They were not happy with what was being taught at the traditional schools. The government pays most of the costs. The parents pay the rest.

Douwe and Dennis put on the costumes they have made especially for this day. They eat breakfast quickly. It is still dark outside when Helen drives them to school.

When Sinterklaas visits the children's school, the boys and girls go up to him, one by one.

All the children have a hard time concentrating today. Nothing special seems to be happening. At noon, Helen comes by the school to pick up the children. Just then, Sinterklaas, Zwarte Piet, and his helpers walk into the classroom. What excitement! Zwarte Piet hands out candies to all the children. Sinterklaas sits down and the children go up to him, one by one.

Sinterklaas and his helpers pose with some of the children.

When it is Douwe's turn, he says his name, and tells Sinterklaas that he has been good. Then Zwarte Piet hands him a small gift. Soon, all the children have spoken to Sinterklaas. Sinterklaas and Zwarte Piet get ready to leave. The children follow them outside and watch as they ride away.

Dennis and Douwe join other children from their school to say goodbye to Sinterklaas and his helpers.

ennis and Douwe are still excited when they arrive back home. Helen reads the boys a story to calm them down. Then she serves them a lunch of vegetable soup and dark rye bread. Dennis, still full of energy, helps his mother with the dishes. When a friend calls, he goes outside to play astronaut. Douwe has a bath, then plays happily on his own. Helen puts Marthe to bed for her afternoon nap and does some housework.

After lunch, Douwe plays happily on his own.

Dennis likes to help his mother around the house, especially before Sinterklaas arrives.

Dennis comes back home in the late afternoon. Helen tells him to wash up. His grandmother and cousins are coming over for dinner and Helen wants him to help her set the table.

After the table is set, all Dennis can think of is Sinterklaas. He can hardly wait to stuff his shoes with carrots for Sinterklaas's horse. When Sinterklaas comes tonight after everyone has gone to bed, he will take the food for his horse. In return, he will leave candy and small gifts in the shoes. He may also leave *speculaas* [SPAY-koo-lahs] in the boys' shoes. These are spicy, dark brown cookies.

Before going to bed, the boys stuff their shoes with carrots and grass for Sinterklaas's horse.

Michel's mother and nephews arrive just before 5:00 p.m. Michel comes home from work a few minutes later. Soon dinner is ready. Helen serves salad and a vegetable lasagna, everyone's favorite meal. The family is vegetarian. For dessert she has baked a special Dutch apple cake. She always uses fresh fruits and vegetables that are <u>organically grown</u>.

Afterwards, everyone gathers around in the living room. Michel lights a fire in the wood stove. While the children open their presents, the adults give each other funny poems they have written. Adults do not exchange gifts until Christmas Day, December 25.

Douwe and Dennis play a game with the new cards their grandmother gave them for St. Nicholas Day.

The boys love their new playing cards, toy cars, and trains. But their favorite gift of all is a puppet theater. The boys begin to talk excitedly about the shows they will put on. Helen lifts Marthe onto the wooden rocking horse she has received. She will be able to sit and rock while she watches the puppet shows.

Douwe and Dennis's favorite present is a puppet theater their parents made for them. Marthe watches their show from her new wooden rocking horse.

Soon it is time for everyone to leave. Tomorrow, St. Nicholas Day, is not a holiday. The children have to go to school. Michel has to go to work. Before going to bed, Dennis and Douwe stuff carrots in their shoes for Sinterklaas's horse. Then Michel and Helen turn off the lights and carry sleepy Marthe upstairs. As the two boys crawl under their covers, they are certain they can hear Sinterklaas and Zwarte Piet talking quietly downstairs.

When Michel read Douwe and Dennis a bedtime story, this is the story he told them.

A long time ago, there lived a little Dutch boy named Hans. Hans was eight years old. He lived with his family in the town of Haarlem. Late one autumn afternoon, he visited a friend who lived on the other side of town. After about an hour, he said goodbye to his friend and started for home.

As he walked back alongside the dike, he noticed how high the water was on the other side. He thought about all the rain that had fallen in the past couple of weeks. Little Hans didn't worry about the water, though. His father was the one who controlled how much water was in the canal. He often talked to Hans about the angry waters from the sea. Way back, when no one controlled the water level, there was lots of flooding. Sometimes people drowned and land was destroyed. Hans knew that wouldn't happen as long as his father was looking after the gates.

He stopped to pick some flowers for his mother. He chased a rabbit that had peeked out of the tall grasses, and he hummed some songs his father had taught him. Suddenly, he noticed that the sun was going down. It was almost dark and he was still a long way from home. He started walking as fast as he could.

Then, Hans heard a strange, gurgling noise. He stopped and looked around. At first Hans couldn't see anything. He looked and he looked. Then he saw what was causing the sound. Water was streaming through a small hole in the dike.

"Oh, no," Hans cried. He didn't know what to do. If he ran for help, the hole might get bigger and bigger. It might even burst and flood the town. He knew what he had to do. Hans threw down his flowers and stuck his finger in the hole in the dike. He called out, "Please, someone, help me." But nobody answered.

After a few minutes, his finger went numb because the water was so cold. He called out for help over and over again, but no one came. Minutes turned into hours. Hans was scared, cold, lonely, and very, very tired. He wanted to sleep more than anything in the world, but he knew he had to stay awake.

At last, the sun came up. In the distance he heard the clomp, clomp of horses. With what little strength he had left, brave Hans shouted, "Help! Over here!" As the horses got closer, Hans called out even louder. A priest jumped out of the buggy and asked Hans what he was doing. "There's a hole in the dike," Hans explained. "Please go to the village and get help."

Soon, all the people from the village came. They wrapped Hans in a blanket and fixed the hole in the dike. Hans was a hero!

WHERE IN THE WORLD IS
THE NETHERLANDS?

The Netherlands is a small country located in northern Europe. Germany lies to the east and Belgium is to the south. The north and west coasts are on the North Sea. The Netherlands also includes a group of islands called the Netherlands Antilles. These islands are across the Atlantic Ocean in the Caribbean.

Despite its northern location, the Netherlands is not cold. The temperature is moderated by a warm ocean current called the Gulf Stream. Winters are usually mild,

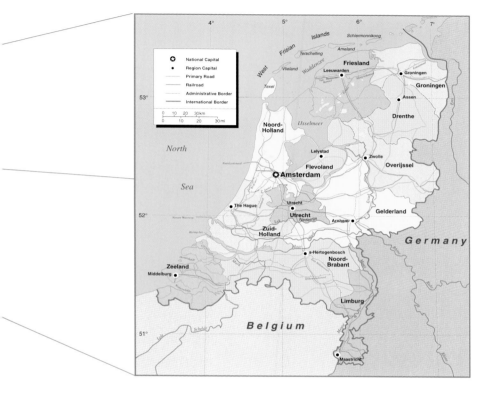

but damp. Summers are warm. The average rainfall is 30 inches (76 cm), which falls throughout the year. The Netherlands is often foggy and very windy because it is on the North Sea.

Land reclamation and overcrowding have disturbed the natural <u>habitats</u> of many plants and animals. The Dutch have created special areas to give these plants and animals a home. Today, small wildlife such as squirrels, foxes, and deer, and ducks, hawks, and cormorants <u>abound</u>.

MORE ABOUT THE NETHERLANDS

Several hundred years ago, the Netherlands was one of the wealthiest nations on earth. During the 1600s, Dutch merchants established trading posts throughout the world. They were among the first people from Europe to settle in New York City. They called the settlement Nieuw Amsterdam (New Amsterdam). Harlem and Brooklyn are named after the Dutch towns of Haarlem and Breukelen.

Even today, the Netherlands is known as a trading nation. It is ideally located on the North Sea and on the estuaries of three major European rivers. Amsterdam has one of Europe's busiest airports. The city of Rotterdam is the largest port in the world.

SOME THINGS TO KNOW ABOUT THE NETHERLANDS

- Amsterdam is the capital.
- The people are called Dutch.
- Most people speak Dutch.
- In school, children learn to speak English, French, and German, in addition to Dutch.
- Dutch money is called the *guilder* [GIL-der].
- Most Dutch are either Roman Catholic or Protestant.
- 99 out of 100 people can read.
- This is the Dutch flag

The Netherlands is sometimes called Holland. But this is just the name of the two most populated provinces, North Holland and South Holland. The name *Netherlands* comes from the word *neder*, which means "low," and *lands*, which means "country."

When many people think of the Netherlands, they think of tulips, windmills, and wooden shoes. Tulips do grow throughout the country, but they are not the only flower that does. At one time, over 10,000 windmills drained water from low-lying land. Today, less than 1,000 windmills remain. Wooden shoes are called *klompen* [KLOM-pen]. They are worn mostly by people in the countryside for gardening or when they are working in wet, muddy fields. *Klompen* keep their feet warm and dry.

One of the most popular winter events takes place only every 8 years or so. That is about how often the ice on the canals freezes thick enough for people to safely skate on it. When that does happen, the Dutch hold a day-long skating race called the Eleven Towns' Race. Several thousand people take part in a 125-mile (200 km) race along canals that link 11 cities in the province of Friesland.

DID YOU KNOW?

The Netherlands has a queen. Her name is Queen Beatrix.

The Netherlands is a modern, well-run country with many different resources. Most people live in towns and cities, but the Netherlands is still the world's third largest exporter of agricultural products. This is because farms are highly mechanized and efficient. Not too many people are farmers, but those who are grow a lot of food and raise a lot of cattle. Most of the vegetables sold in Europe come from greenhouses in the Netherlands.

The Netherlands is also famous for cheese and flowers. Over a quarter of the cheese sold around the world comes from here. At least half of the world's exported flowers come from the Netherlands. Millions of flowers and plants are sold every day at flower auctions.

DID YOU KNOW?

The Netherlands has about 9,375 miles (about 15,000 km) of bicycle paths. Compare that to the distance between New York and Los Angeles, which is about 2,500 miles (4,000 km). That's a lot of bike paths!

Soccer, which the Dutch call *voetbal* [VOOT-ball], is the most popular sport. Many people play tennis. Walking, bicycling, volleyball, and ice skating are also favorite activities.

Some of the world's most famous artists are Dutch. Rembrandt, Vermeer, and Van Gogh are perhaps the best known.

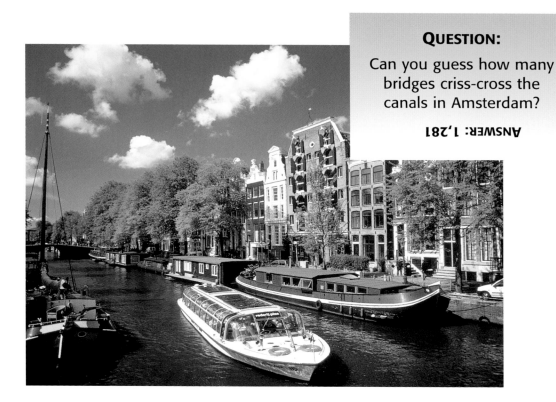

GLOSSARY

abound: to have a large amount of something

auction: a sale where goods are sold to the person who offers the most money for them

canal: a human-made waterway

dike: a hill made of earth to stop water from flooding land

concentrate: to focus or direct one's efforts or thoughts toward something

environment: the natural world

estuary: the wide mouth of a river where it meets an ocean or lake

habitat: the place where a plant or an animal lives

industrial: to do with businesses and factories

Moor: a person of Arab descent from North West Africa

nature: all things except those made by people

organically grown: a way of raising plants without using fertilizers or pesticides

reclaim: make usable again

sea wall: a wall built along the shore to hold back the sea or ocean

seepage: a slow, constant leaking of liquid

stump: the part of a tree that stays in the ground after the tree has been cut down

traveling companion: a person who goes with someone when they travel

wade: to walk in shallow water